INTERNET PASSWORD BOOK

VOL. 2

THIS BOOK BELONGS TO:

____

____

____

____

ISBN-13: 978-1721702688
ISBN-10: 1721702687

NOTE

Internet Service Provider

Account Number:

Tech Support Number:

Customer Service Number:

Email Account

Username:

Password:

Broadband Modem

Model Number:

Serial Number:

Mac Address:

Administration URL/IP Address:

WAN IP Address:

Username:

Password:

Router/Wireless Access Point

Model Number:

Serial Number:

Default Admin IP Address:

Default Username:

Default Password:

User Default URL/IP Address:

User Default Username:

User Default Password:

Notes

Date:

Website:

Username:

Password:

Email:

Phone:

Security questions:

Notes:

◊ ◊ ◊ ◊ ◊ ◊ ◊ ◊ ◊ ◊ ◊ ◊ ◊ ◊ ◊ ◊ ◊

Date:

Website:

Username:

Password:

Email:

Phone:

Security questions:

Notes:

◊ ◊ ◊ ◊ ◊ ◊ ◊ ◊ ◊ ◊ ◊ ◊ ◊ ◊ ◊ ◊ ◊

Date:

Website:

Username:

Password:

Email:

Phone:

Security questions:

Notes:

Date:
Website:
Username:
Password:
Email:
Phone:
Security questions:
Notes:

◊ ◊ ◊ ◊ ◊ ◊ ◊ ◊ ◊ ◊ ◊ ◊ ◊ ◊ ◊ ◊

Date:
Website:
Username:
Password:
Email:
Phone:
Security questions:
Notes:

◊ ◊ ◊ ◊ ◊ ◊ ◊ ◊ ◊ ◊ ◊ ◊ ◊ ◊ ◊ ◊

Date:
Website:
Username:
Password:
Email:
Phone:
Security questions:
Notes:

Date:

Website:

Username:

Password:

Email:

Phone:

Security questions:

Notes:

◇ ◇ ◇ ◇ ◇ ◇ ◇ ◇ ◇ ◇ ◇ ◇ ◇ ◇ ◇

Date:

Website:

Username:

Password:

Email:

Phone:

Security questions:

Notes:

◇ ◇ ◇ ◇ ◇ ◇ ◇ ◇ ◇ ◇ ◇ ◇ ◇ ◇ ◇

Date:

Website:

Username:

Password:

Email:

Phone:

Security questions:

Notes:

Date:

Website:

Username:

Password:

Email:

Phone:

Security questions:

Notes:

◊ ◊ ◊ ◊ ◊ ◊ ◊ ◊ ◊ ◊ ◊ ◊ ◊ ◊ ◊ ◊

Date:

Website:

Username:

Password:

Email:

Phone:

Security questions:

Notes:

◊ ◊ ◊ ◊ ◊ ◊ ◊ ◊ ◊ ◊ ◊ ◊ ◊ ◊ ◊ ◊

Date:

Website:

Username:

Password:

Email:

Phone:

Security questions:

Notes:

Date:

Website:

Username:

Password:

Email:

Phone:

Security questions:

Notes:

◇ ◇ ◇ ◇ ◇ ◇ ◇ ◇ ◇ ◇ ◇ ◇ ◇ ◇ ◇ ◇

Date:

Website:

Username:

Password:

Email:

Phone:

Security questions:

Notes:

◇ ◇ ◇ ◇ ◇ ◇ ◇ ◇ ◇ ◇ ◇ ◇ ◇ ◇ ◇ ◇

Date:

Website:

Username:

Password:

Email:

Phone:

Security questions:

Notes:

Date:

Website:

Username:

Password:

Email:

Phone:

Security questions:

Notes:

◇ ◇ ◇ ◇ ◇ ◇ ◇ ◇ ◇ ◇ ◇ ◇ ◇ ◇ ◇ ◇

Date:

Website:

Username:

Password:

Email:

Phone:

Security questions:

Notes:

◇ ◇ ◇ ◇ ◇ ◇ ◇ ◇ ◇ ◇ ◇ ◇ ◇ ◇ ◇ ◇

Date:

Website:

Username:

Password:

Email:

Phone:

Security questions:

Notes:

Date:

Website:

Username:

Password:

Email:

Phone:

Security questions:

Notes:

◊ ◊ ◊ ◊ ◊ ◊ ◊ ◊ ◊ ◊ ◊ ◊ ◊ ◊ ◊ ◊ ◊

Date:

Website:

Username:

Password:

Email:

Phone:

Security questions:

Notes:

◊ ◊ ◊ ◊ ◊ ◊ ◊ ◊ ◊ ◊ ◊ ◊ ◊ ◊ ◊ ◊ ◊

Date:

Website:

Username:

Password:

Email:

Phone:

Security questions:

Notes:

Date:

Website:

Username:

Password:

Email:

Phone:

Security questions:

Notes:

◇ ◇ ◇ ◇ ◇ ◇ ◇ ◇ ◇ ◇ ◇ ◇ ◇ ◇ ◇ ◇

Date:

Website:

Username:

Password:

Email:

Phone:

Security questions:

Notes:

◇ ◇ ◇ ◇ ◇ ◇ ◇ ◇ ◇ ◇ ◇ ◇ ◇ ◇ ◇ ◇

Date:

Website:

Username:

Password:

Email:

Phone:

Security questions:

Notes:

Date:
Website:
Username:
Password:
Email:
Phone:
Security questions:
Notes:

◇ ◇ ◇ ◇ ◇ ◇ ◇ ◇ ◇ ◇ ◇ ◇ ◇ ◇ ◇

Date:
Website:
Username:
Password:
Email:
Phone:
Security questions:
Notes:

◇ ◇ ◇ ◇ ◇ ◇ ◇ ◇ ◇ ◇ ◇ ◇ ◇ ◇ ◇

Date:
Website:
Username:
Password:
Email:
Phone:
Security questions:
Notes:

Date:

Website:

Username:

Password:

Email:

Phone:

Security questions:

Notes:

◇ ◇ ◇ ◇ ◇ ◇ ◇ ◇ ◇ ◇ ◇ ◇ ◇ ◇ ◇ ◇

Date:

Website:

Username:

Password:

Email:

Phone:

Security questions:

Notes:

◇ ◇ ◇ ◇ ◇ ◇ ◇ ◇ ◇ ◇ ◇ ◇ ◇ ◇ ◇ ◇

Date:

Website:

Username:

Password:

Email:

Phone:

Security questions:

Notes:

Date:

Website:

Username:

Password:

Email:

Phone:

Security questions:

Notes:

◊ ◊ ◊ ◊ ◊ ◊ ◊ ◊ ◊ ◊ ◊ ◊ ◊ ◊ ◊ ◊

Date:

Website:

Username:

Password:

Email:

Phone:

Security questions:

Notes:

◊ ◊ ◊ ◊ ◊ ◊ ◊ ◊ ◊ ◊ ◊ ◊ ◊ ◊ ◊ ◊

Date:

Website:

Username:

Password:

Email:

Phone:

Security questions:

Notes:

Date:

Website:

Username:

Password:

Email:

Phone:

Security questions:

Notes:

◊ ◊ ◊ ◊ ◊ ◊ ◊ ◊ ◊ ◊ ◊ ◊ ◊ ◊ ◊ ◊ ◊

Date:

Website:

Username:

Password:

Email:

Phone:

Security questions:

Notes:

◊ ◊ ◊ ◊ ◊ ◊ ◊ ◊ ◊ ◊ ◊ ◊ ◊ ◊ ◊ ◊ ◊

Date:

Website:

Username:

Password:

Email:

Phone:

Security questions:

Notes:

Date:
Website:
Username:
Password:
Email:
Phone:
Security questions:
Notes:

◇ ◇ ◇ ◇ ◇ ◇ ◇ ◇ ◇ ◇ ◇ ◇ ◇ ◇ ◇ ◇

Date:
Website:
Username:
Password:
Email:
Phone:
Security questions:
Notes:

◇ ◇ ◇ ◇ ◇ ◇ ◇ ◇ ◇ ◇ ◇ ◇ ◇ ◇ ◇ ◇

Date:
Website:
Username:
Password:
Email:
Phone:
Security questions:
Notes:

Date:

Website:

Username:

Password:

Email:

Phone:

Security questions:

Notes:

◇ ◇ ◇ ◇ ◇ ◇ ◇ ◇ ◇ ◇ ◇ ◇ ◇ ◇ ◇ ◇

Date:

Website:

Username:

Password:

Email:

Phone:

Security questions:

Notes:

◇ ◇ ◇ ◇ ◇ ◇ ◇ ◇ ◇ ◇ ◇ ◇ ◇ ◇ ◇ ◇

Date:

Website:

Username:

Password:

Email:

Phone:

Security questions:

Notes:

Date:

Website:

Username:

Password:

Email:

Phone:

Security questions:

Notes:

◇ ◇ ◇ ◇ ◇ ◇ ◇ ◇ ◇ ◇ ◇ ◇ ◇ ◇ ◇ ◇

Date:

Website:

Username:

Password:

Email:

Phone:

Security questions:

Notes:

◇ ◇ ◇ ◇ ◇ ◇ ◇ ◇ ◇ ◇ ◇ ◇ ◇ ◇ ◇ ◇

Date:

Website:

Username:

Password:

Email:

Phone:

Security questions:

Notes:

Date:

Website:

Username:

Password:

Email:

Phone:

Security questions:

Notes:

◊ ◊ ◊ ◊ ◊ ◊ ◊ ◊ ◊ ◊ ◊ ◊ ◊ ◊ ◊ ◊

Date:

Website:

Username:

Password:

Email:

Phone:

Security questions:

Notes:

◊ ◊ ◊ ◊ ◊ ◊ ◊ ◊ ◊ ◊ ◊ ◊ ◊ ◊ ◊ ◊

Date:

Website:

Username:

Password:

Email:

Phone:

Security questions:

Notes:

Date:

Website:

Username:

Password:

Email:

Phone:

Security questions:

Notes:

◊ ◊ ◊ ◊ ◊ ◊ ◊ ◊ ◊ ◊ ◊ ◊ ◊ ◊ ◊ ◊ ◊

Date:

Website:

Username:

Password:

Email:

Phone:

Security questions:

Notes:

◊ ◊ ◊ ◊ ◊ ◊ ◊ ◊ ◊ ◊ ◊ ◊ ◊ ◊ ◊ ◊ ◊

Date:

Website:

Username:

Password:

Email:

Phone:

Security questions:

Notes:

Date:

Website:

Username:

Password:

Email:

Phone:

Security questions:

Notes:

◊ ◊ ◊ ◊ ◊ ◊ ◊ ◊ ◊ ◊ ◊ ◊ ◊ ◊ ◊ ◊ ◊

Date:

Website:

Username:

Password:

Email:

Phone:

Security questions:

Notes:

◊ ◊ ◊ ◊ ◊ ◊ ◊ ◊ ◊ ◊ ◊ ◊ ◊ ◊ ◊ ◊ ◊

Date:

Website:

Username:

Password:

Email:

Phone:

Security questions:

Notes:

Date:

Website:

Username:

Password:

Email:

Phone:

Security questions:

Notes:

◇ ◇ ◇ ◇ ◇ ◇ ◇ ◇ ◇ ◇ ◇ ◇ ◇ ◇ ◇ ◇

Date:

Website:

Username:

Password:

Email:

Phone:

Security questions:

Notes:

◇ ◇ ◇ ◇ ◇ ◇ ◇ ◇ ◇ ◇ ◇ ◇ ◇ ◇ ◇ ◇

Date:

Website:

Username:

Password:

Email:

Phone:

Security questions:

Notes:

Date: ....
Website: ....
Username: ....
Password: ....
Email: ....
Phone: ....
Security questions: ....
Notes: ....
....

◊ ◊ ◊ ◊ ◊ ◊ ◊ ◊ ◊ ◊ ◊ ◊ ◊ ◊ ◊ ◊ ◊

Date: ....
Website: ....
Username: ....
Password: ....
Email: ....
Phone: ....
Security questions: ....
Notes: ....
....

◊ ◊ ◊ ◊ ◊ ◊ ◊ ◊ ◊ ◊ ◊ ◊ ◊ ◊ ◊ ◊ ◊

Date: ....
Website: ....
Username: ....
Password: ....
Email: ....
Phone: ....
Security questions: ....
Notes: ....
....

Date:

Website:

Username:

Password:

Email:

Phone:

Security questions:

Notes:

◊ ◊ ◊ ◊ ◊ ◊ ◊ ◊ ◊ ◊ ◊ ◊ ◊ ◊ ◊ ◊ ◊

Date:

Website:

Username:

Password:

Email:

Phone:

Security questions:

Notes:

◊ ◊ ◊ ◊ ◊ ◊ ◊ ◊ ◊ ◊ ◊ ◊ ◊ ◊ ◊ ◊ ◊

Date:

Website:

Username:

Password:

Email:

Phone:

Security questions:

Notes:

Date:

Website:

Username:

Password:

Email:

Phone:

Security questions:

Notes:

◊ ◊ ◊ ◊ ◊ ◊ ◊ ◊ ◊ ◊ ◊ ◊ ◊ ◊ ◊ ◊

Date:

Website:

Username:

Password:

Email:

Phone:

Security questions:

Notes:

◊ ◊ ◊ ◊ ◊ ◊ ◊ ◊ ◊ ◊ ◊ ◊ ◊ ◊ ◊ ◊

Date:

Website:

Username:

Password:

Email:

Phone:

Security questions:

Notes:

Date:
Website:
Username:
Password:
Email:
Phone:
Security questions:
Notes:

◊ ◊ ◊ ◊ ◊ ◊ ◊ ◊ ◊ ◊ ◊ ◊ ◊ ◊ ◊ ◊

Date:
Website:
Username:
Password:
Email:
Phone:
Security questions:
Notes:

◊ ◊ ◊ ◊ ◊ ◊ ◊ ◊ ◊ ◊ ◊ ◊ ◊ ◊ ◊ ◊

Date:
Website:
Username:
Password:
Email:
Phone:
Security questions:
Notes:

Date:

Website:

Username:

Password:

Email:

Phone:

Security questions:

Notes:

◇ ◇ ◇ ◇ ◇ ◇ ◇ ◇ ◇ ◇ ◇ ◇ ◇ ◇ ◇ ◇ ◇

Date:

Website:

Username:

Password:

Email:

Phone:

Security questions:

Notes:

◇ ◇ ◇ ◇ ◇ ◇ ◇ ◇ ◇ ◇ ◇ ◇ ◇ ◇ ◇ ◇ ◇

Date:

Website:

Username:

Password:

Email:

Phone:

Security questions:

Notes:

Date:
Website:
Username:
Password:
Email:
Phone:
Security questions:
Notes:

◇ ◇ ◇ ◇ ◇ ◇ ◇ ◇ ◇ ◇ ◇ ◇ ◇ ◇ ◇ ◇

Date:
Website:
Username:
Password:
Email:
Phone:
Security questions:
Notes:

◇ ◇ ◇ ◇ ◇ ◇ ◇ ◇ ◇ ◇ ◇ ◇ ◇ ◇ ◇ ◇

Date:
Website:
Username:
Password:
Email:
Phone:
Security questions:
Notes:

Date:
Website:
Username:
Password:
Email:
Phone:
Security questions:
Notes:

◇ ◇ ◇ ◇ ◇ ◇ ◇ ◇ ◇ ◇ ◇ ◇ ◇ ◇ ◇ ◇

Date:
Website:
Username:
Password:
Email:
Phone:
Security questions:
Notes:

◇ ◇ ◇ ◇ ◇ ◇ ◇ ◇ ◇ ◇ ◇ ◇ ◇ ◇ ◇ ◇

Date:
Website:
Username:
Password:
Email:
Phone:
Security questions:
Notes:

Date:

Website:

Username:

Password:

Email:

Phone:

Security questions:

Notes:

◇ ◇ ◇ ◇ ◇ ◇ ◇ ◇ ◇ ◇ ◇ ◇ ◇ ◇ ◇ ◇

Date:

Website:

Username:

Password:

Email:

Phone:

Security questions:

Notes:

◇ ◇ ◇ ◇ ◇ ◇ ◇ ◇ ◇ ◇ ◇ ◇ ◇ ◇ ◇ ◇

Date:

Website:

Username:

Password:

Email:

Phone:

Security questions:

Notes:

Date:
Website:
Username:
Password:
Email:
Phone:
Security questions:
Notes:

◇ ◇ ◇ ◇ ◇ ◇ ◇ ◇ ◇ ◇ ◇ ◇ ◇ ◇ ◇ ◇

Date:
Website:
Username:
Password:
Email:
Phone:
Security questions:
Notes:

◇ ◇ ◇ ◇ ◇ ◇ ◇ ◇ ◇ ◇ ◇ ◇ ◇ ◇ ◇ ◇

Date:
Website:
Username:
Password:
Email:
Phone:
Security questions:
Notes:

Date:
Website:
Username:
Password:
Email:
Phone:
Security questions:
Notes:

◊ ◊ ◊ ◊ ◊ ◊ ◊ ◊ ◊ ◊ ◊ ◊ ◊ ◊ ◊ ◊ ◊

Date:
Website:
Username:
Password:
Email:
Phone:
Security questions:
Notes:

◊ ◊ ◊ ◊ ◊ ◊ ◊ ◊ ◊ ◊ ◊ ◊ ◊ ◊ ◊ ◊ ◊

Date:
Website:
Username:
Password:
Email:
Phone:
Security questions:
Notes:

Date:

Website:

Username:

Password:

Email:

Phone:

Security questions:

Notes:

◊ ◊ ◊ ◊ ◊ ◊ ◊ ◊ ◊ ◊ ◊ ◊ ◊ ◊ ◊ ◊

Date:

Website:

Username:

Password:

Email:

Phone:

Security questions:

Notes:

◊ ◊ ◊ ◊ ◊ ◊ ◊ ◊ ◊ ◊ ◊ ◊ ◊ ◊ ◊ ◊

Date:

Website:

Username:

Password:

Email:

Phone:

Security questions:

Notes:

Date:

Website:

Username:

Password:

Email:

Phone:

Security questions:

Notes:

◊ ◊ ◊ ◊ ◊ ◊ ◊ ◊ ◊ ◊ ◊ ◊ ◊ ◊ ◊ ◊

Date:

Website:

Username:

Password:

Email:

Phone:

Security questions:

Notes:

◊ ◊ ◊ ◊ ◊ ◊ ◊ ◊ ◊ ◊ ◊ ◊ ◊ ◊ ◊ ◊

Date:

Website:

Username:

Password:

Email:

Phone:

Security questions:

Notes:

Date: ....

Website: ....

Username: ....

Password: ....

Email: ....

Phone: ....

Security questions: ....

Notes: ....

....

◇ ◇ ◇ ◇ ◇ ◇ ◇ ◇ ◇ ◇ ◇ ◇ ◇ ◇ ◇ ◇ ◇

Date: ....

Website: ....

Username: ....

Password: ....

Email: ....

Phone: ....

Security questions: ....

Notes: ....

....

◇ ◇ ◇ ◇ ◇ ◇ ◇ ◇ ◇ ◇ ◇ ◇ ◇ ◇ ◇ ◇ ◇

Date: ....

Website: ....

Username: ....

Password: ....

Email: ....

Phone: ....

Security questions: ....

Notes: ....

....

Date:
Website:
Username:
Password:
Email:
Phone:
Security questions:
Notes:

◇ ◇ ◇ ◇ ◇ ◇ ◇ ◇ ◇ ◇ ◇ ◇ ◇ ◇ ◇ ◇

Date:
Website:
Username:
Password:
Email:
Phone:
Security questions:
Notes:

◇ ◇ ◇ ◇ ◇ ◇ ◇ ◇ ◇ ◇ ◇ ◇ ◇ ◇ ◇ ◇

Date:
Website:
Username:
Password:
Email:
Phone:
Security questions:
Notes:

Date:
Website:
Username:
Password:
Email:
Phone:
Security questions:
Notes:

◊ ◊ ◊ ◊ ◊ ◊ ◊ ◊ ◊ ◊ ◊ ◊ ◊ ◊ ◊ ◊ ◊

Date:
Website:
Username:
Password:
Email:
Phone:
Security questions:
Notes:

◊ ◊ ◊ ◊ ◊ ◊ ◊ ◊ ◊ ◊ ◊ ◊ ◊ ◊ ◊ ◊ ◊

Date:
Website:
Username:
Password:
Email:
Phone:
Security questions:
Notes:

Date: ....
Website: ....
Username: ....
Password: ....
Email: ....
Phone: ....
Security questions: ....
Notes: ....

....

◊ ◊ ◊ ◊ ◊ ◊ ◊ ◊ ◊ ◊ ◊ ◊ ◊ ◊ ◊ ◊ ◊

Date: ....
Website: ....
Username: ....
Password: ....
Email: ....
Phone: ....
Security questions: ....
Notes: ....

....

◊ ◊ ◊ ◊ ◊ ◊ ◊ ◊ ◊ ◊ ◊ ◊ ◊ ◊ ◊ ◊ ◊

Date: ....
Website: ....
Username: ....
Password: ....
Email: ....
Phone: ....
Security questions: ....
Notes: ....

....

Date:
Website:
Username:
Password:
Email:
Phone:
Security questions:
Notes:

◊ ◊ ◊ ◊ ◊ ◊ ◊ ◊ ◊ ◊ ◊ ◊ ◊ ◊ ◊ ◊

Date:
Website:
Username:
Password:
Email:
Phone:
Security questions:
Notes:

◊ ◊ ◊ ◊ ◊ ◊ ◊ ◊ ◊ ◊ ◊ ◊ ◊ ◊ ◊ ◊

Date:
Website:
Username:
Password:
Email:
Phone:
Security questions:
Notes:

Date:
Website:
Username:
Password:
Email:
Phone:
Security questions:
Notes:

◊ ◊ ◊ ◊ ◊ ◊ ◊ ◊ ◊ ◊ ◊ ◊ ◊ ◊ ◊ ◊ ◊

Date:
Website:
Username:
Password:
Email:
Phone:
Security questions:
Notes:

◊ ◊ ◊ ◊ ◊ ◊ ◊ ◊ ◊ ◊ ◊ ◊ ◊ ◊ ◊ ◊ ◊

Date:
Website:
Username:
Password:
Email:
Phone:
Security questions:
Notes:

Date:

Website:

Username:

Password:

Email:

Phone:

Security questions:

Notes:

◇ ◇ ◇ ◇ ◇ ◇ ◇ ◇ ◇ ◇ ◇ ◇ ◇ ◇ ◇ ◇ ◇

Date:

Website:

Username:

Password:

Email:

Phone:

Security questions:

Notes:

◇ ◇ ◇ ◇ ◇ ◇ ◇ ◇ ◇ ◇ ◇ ◇ ◇ ◇ ◇ ◇ ◇

Date:

Website:

Username:

Password:

Email:

Phone:

Security questions:

Notes:

Date:

Website:

Username:

Password:

Email:

Phone:

Security questions:

Notes:

◇ ◇ ◇ ◇ ◇ ◇ ◇ ◇ ◇ ◇ ◇ ◇ ◇ ◇ ◇ ◇ ◇

Date:

Website:

Username:

Password:

Email:

Phone:

Security questions:

Notes:

◇ ◇ ◇ ◇ ◇ ◇ ◇ ◇ ◇ ◇ ◇ ◇ ◇ ◇ ◇ ◇ ◇

Date:

Website:

Username:

Password:

Email:

Phone:

Security questions:

Notes:

Date:
Website:
Username:
Password:
Email:
Phone:
Security questions:
Notes:

◊ ◊ ◊ ◊ ◊ ◊ ◊ ◊ ◊ ◊ ◊ ◊ ◊ ◊ ◊ ◊ ◊

Date:
Website:
Username:
Password:
Email:
Phone:
Security questions:
Notes:

◊ ◊ ◊ ◊ ◊ ◊ ◊ ◊ ◊ ◊ ◊ ◊ ◊ ◊ ◊ ◊ ◊

Date:
Website:
Username:
Password:
Email:
Phone:
Security questions:
Notes:

Date:

Website:

Username:

Password:

Email:

Phone:

Security questions:

Notes:

◊ ◊ ◊ ◊ ◊ ◊ ◊ ◊ ◊ ◊ ◊ ◊ ◊ ◊ ◊ ◊

Date:

Website:

Username:

Password:

Email:

Phone:

Security questions:

Notes:

◊ ◊ ◊ ◊ ◊ ◊ ◊ ◊ ◊ ◊ ◊ ◊ ◊ ◊ ◊ ◊

Date:

Website:

Username:

Password:

Email:

Phone:

Security questions:

Notes:

Date:

Website:

Username:

Password:

Email:

Phone:

Security questions:

Notes:

◇ ◇ ◇ ◇ ◇ ◇ ◇ ◇ ◇ ◇ ◇ ◇ ◇ ◇ ◇ ◇

Date:

Website:

Username:

Password:

Email:

Phone:

Security questions:

Notes:

◇ ◇ ◇ ◇ ◇ ◇ ◇ ◇ ◇ ◇ ◇ ◇ ◇ ◇ ◇ ◇

Date:

Website:

Username:

Password:

Email:

Phone:

Security questions:

Notes:

Date:

Website:

Username:

Password:

Email:

Phone:

Security questions:

Notes:

◊ ◊ ◊ ◊ ◊ ◊ ◊ ◊ ◊ ◊ ◊ ◊ ◊ ◊ ◊ ◊ ◊

Date:

Website:

Username:

Password:

Email:

Phone:

Security questions:

Notes:

◊ ◊ ◊ ◊ ◊ ◊ ◊ ◊ ◊ ◊ ◊ ◊ ◊ ◊ ◊ ◊ ◊

Date:

Website:

Username:

Password:

Email:

Phone:

Security questions:

Notes:

Date:
Website:
Username:
Password:
Email:
Phone:
Security questions:
Notes:

◇ ◇ ◇ ◇ ◇ ◇ ◇ ◇ ◇ ◇ ◇ ◇ ◇ ◇ ◇

Date:
Website:
Username:
Password:
Email:
Phone:
Security questions:
Notes:

◇ ◇ ◇ ◇ ◇ ◇ ◇ ◇ ◇ ◇ ◇ ◇ ◇ ◇ ◇

Date:
Website:
Username:
Password:
Email:
Phone:
Security questions:
Notes:

Date:

Website:

Username:

Password:

Email:

Phone:

Security questions:

Notes:

◊ ◊ ◊ ◊ ◊ ◊ ◊ ◊ ◊ ◊ ◊ ◊ ◊ ◊ ◊ ◊ ◊

Date:

Website:

Username:

Password:

Email:

Phone:

Security questions:

Notes:

◊ ◊ ◊ ◊ ◊ ◊ ◊ ◊ ◊ ◊ ◊ ◊ ◊ ◊ ◊ ◊ ◊

Date:

Website:

Username:

Password:

Email:

Phone:

Security questions:

Notes:

Date:

Website:

Username:

Password:

Email:

Phone:

Security questions:

Notes:

◇ ◇ ◇ ◇ ◇ ◇ ◇ ◇ ◇ ◇ ◇ ◇ ◇ ◇ ◇ ◇ ◇

Date:

Website:

Username:

Password:

Email:

Phone:

Security questions:

Notes:

◇ ◇ ◇ ◇ ◇ ◇ ◇ ◇ ◇ ◇ ◇ ◇ ◇ ◇ ◇ ◇ ◇

Date:

Website:

Username:

Password:

Email:

Phone:

Security questions:

Notes:

Date:
Website:
Username:
Password:
Email:
Phone:
Security questions:
Notes:

◇ ◇ ◇ ◇ ◇ ◇ ◇ ◇ ◇ ◇ ◇ ◇ ◇ ◇ ◇ ◇

Date:
Website:
Username:
Password:
Email:
Phone:
Security questions:
Notes:

◇ ◇ ◇ ◇ ◇ ◇ ◇ ◇ ◇ ◇ ◇ ◇ ◇ ◇ ◇ ◇

Date:
Website:
Username:
Password:
Email:
Phone:
Security questions:
Notes:

Date:
Website:
Username:
Password:
Email:
Phone:
Security questions:
Notes:

◊ ◊ ◊ ◊ ◊ ◊ ◊ ◊ ◊ ◊ ◊ ◊ ◊ ◊ ◊ ◊

Date:
Website:
Username:
Password:
Email:
Phone:
Security questions:
Notes:

◊ ◊ ◊ ◊ ◊ ◊ ◊ ◊ ◊ ◊ ◊ ◊ ◊ ◊ ◊ ◊

Date:
Website:
Username:
Password:
Email:
Phone:
Security questions:
Notes:

Date: ....
Website: ....
Username: ....
Password: ....
Email: ....
Phone: ....
Security questions: ....
Notes: ....
....

◇ ◇ ◇ ◇ ◇ ◇ ◇ ◇ ◇ ◇ ◇ ◇ ◇ ◇ ◇ ◇

Date: ....
Website: ....
Username: ....
Password: ....
Email: ....
Phone: ....
Security questions: ....
Notes: ....
....

◇ ◇ ◇ ◇ ◇ ◇ ◇ ◇ ◇ ◇ ◇ ◇ ◇ ◇ ◇ ◇

Date: ....
Website: ....
Username: ....
Password: ....
Email: ....
Phone: ....
Security questions: ....
Notes: ....
....

Date:
Website:
Username:
Password:
Email:
Phone:
Security questions:
Notes:

◊ ◊ ◊ ◊ ◊ ◊ ◊ ◊ ◊ ◊ ◊ ◊ ◊ ◊ ◊ ◊

Date:
Website:
Username:
Password:
Email:
Phone:
Security questions:
Notes:

◊ ◊ ◊ ◊ ◊ ◊ ◊ ◊ ◊ ◊ ◊ ◊ ◊ ◊ ◊ ◊

Date:
Website:
Username:
Password:
Email:
Phone:
Security questions:
Notes:

Date:

Website:

Username:

Password:

Email:

Phone:

Security questions:

Notes:

◊ ◊ ◊ ◊ ◊ ◊ ◊ ◊ ◊ ◊ ◊ ◊ ◊ ◊ ◊ ◊

Date:

Website:

Username:

Password:

Email:

Phone:

Security questions:

Notes:

◊ ◊ ◊ ◊ ◊ ◊ ◊ ◊ ◊ ◊ ◊ ◊ ◊ ◊ ◊ ◊

Date:

Website:

Username:

Password:

Email:

Phone:

Security questions:

Notes:

Date:

Website:

Username:

Password:

Email:

Phone:

Security questions:

Notes:

◇ ◇ ◇ ◇ ◇ ◇ ◇ ◇ ◇ ◇ ◇ ◇ ◇ ◇ ◇

Date:

Website:

Username:

Password:

Email:

Phone:

Security questions:

Notes:

◇ ◇ ◇ ◇ ◇ ◇ ◇ ◇ ◇ ◇ ◇ ◇ ◇ ◇ ◇

Date:

Website:

Username:

Password:

Email:

Phone:

Security questions:

Notes:

Date:

Website:

Username:

Password:

Email:

Phone:

Security questions:

Notes:

◊ ◊ ◊ ◊ ◊ ◊ ◊ ◊ ◊ ◊ ◊ ◊ ◊ ◊ ◊ ◊

Date:

Website:

Username:

Password:

Email:

Phone:

Security questions:

Notes:

◊ ◊ ◊ ◊ ◊ ◊ ◊ ◊ ◊ ◊ ◊ ◊ ◊ ◊ ◊ ◊

Date:

Website:

Username:

Password:

Email:

Phone:

Security questions:

Notes:

Date:
Website:
Username:
Password:
Email:
Phone:
Security questions:
Notes:

◇ ◇ ◇ ◇ ◇ ◇ ◇ ◇ ◇ ◇ ◇ ◇ ◇ ◇ ◇

Date:
Website:
Username:
Password:
Email:
Phone:
Security questions:
Notes:

◇ ◇ ◇ ◇ ◇ ◇ ◇ ◇ ◇ ◇ ◇ ◇ ◇ ◇ ◇

Date:
Website:
Username:
Password:
Email:
Phone:
Security questions:
Notes:

Date:

Website:

Username:

Password:

Email:

Phone:

Security questions:

Notes:

◇ ◇ ◇ ◇ ◇ ◇ ◇ ◇ ◇ ◇ ◇ ◇ ◇ ◇ ◇ ◇

Date:

Website:

Username:

Password:

Email:

Phone:

Security questions:

Notes:

◇ ◇ ◇ ◇ ◇ ◇ ◇ ◇ ◇ ◇ ◇ ◇ ◇ ◇ ◇ ◇

Date:

Website:

Username:

Password:

Email:

Phone:

Security questions:

Notes:

Date:

Website:

Username:

Password:

Email:

Phone:

Security questions:

Notes:

◇ ◇ ◇ ◇ ◇ ◇ ◇ ◇ ◇ ◇ ◇ ◇ ◇ ◇ ◇ ◇

Date:

Website:

Username:

Password:

Email:

Phone:

Security questions:

Notes:

◇ ◇ ◇ ◇ ◇ ◇ ◇ ◇ ◇ ◇ ◇ ◇ ◇ ◇ ◇ ◇

Date:

Website:

Username:

Password:

Email:

Phone:

Security questions:

Notes:

Date:

Website:

Username:

Password:

Email:

Phone:

Security questions:

Notes:

◊ ◊ ◊ ◊ ◊ ◊ ◊ ◊ ◊ ◊ ◊ ◊ ◊ ◊ ◊ ◊ ◊

Date:

Website:

Username:

Password:

Email:

Phone:

Security questions:

Notes:

◊ ◊ ◊ ◊ ◊ ◊ ◊ ◊ ◊ ◊ ◊ ◊ ◊ ◊ ◊ ◊ ◊

Date:

Website:

Username:

Password:

Email:

Phone:

Security questions:

Notes:

Date:

Website:

Username:

Password:

Email:

Phone:

Security questions:

Notes:

◇ ◇ ◇ ◇ ◇ ◇ ◇ ◇ ◇ ◇ ◇ ◇ ◇ ◇ ◇ ◇

Date:

Website:

Username:

Password:

Email:

Phone:

Security questions:

Notes:

◇ ◇ ◇ ◇ ◇ ◇ ◇ ◇ ◇ ◇ ◇ ◇ ◇ ◇ ◇ ◇

Date:

Website:

Username:

Password:

Email:

Phone:

Security questions:

Notes:

Date:
Website:
Username:
Password:
Email:
Phone:
Security questions:
Notes:

◊ ◊ ◊ ◊ ◊ ◊ ◊ ◊ ◊ ◊ ◊ ◊ ◊ ◊ ◊ ◊

Date:
Website:
Username:
Password:
Email:
Phone:
Security questions:
Notes:

◊ ◊ ◊ ◊ ◊ ◊ ◊ ◊ ◊ ◊ ◊ ◊ ◊ ◊ ◊ ◊

Date:
Website:
Username:
Password:
Email:
Phone:
Security questions:
Notes:

Date:

Website:

Username:

Password:

Email:

Phone:

Security questions:

Notes:

◊ ◊ ◊ ◊ ◊ ◊ ◊ ◊ ◊ ◊ ◊ ◊ ◊ ◊ ◊ ◊

Date:

Website:

Username:

Password:

Email:

Phone:

Security questions:

Notes:

◊ ◊ ◊ ◊ ◊ ◊ ◊ ◊ ◊ ◊ ◊ ◊ ◊ ◊ ◊ ◊

Date:

Website:

Username:

Password:

Email:

Phone:

Security questions:

Notes:

Date:
Website:
Username:
Password:
Email:
Phone:
Security questions:
Notes:

◇ ◇ ◇ ◇ ◇ ◇ ◇ ◇ ◇ ◇ ◇ ◇ ◇ ◇ ◇ ◇

Date:
Website:
Username:
Password:
Email:
Phone:
Security questions:
Notes:

◇ ◇ ◇ ◇ ◇ ◇ ◇ ◇ ◇ ◇ ◇ ◇ ◇ ◇ ◇ ◇

Date:
Website:
Username:
Password:
Email:
Phone:
Security questions:
Notes:

Date:
Website:
Username:
Password:
Email:
Phone:
Security questions:
Notes:

◊ ◊ ◊ ◊ ◊ ◊ ◊ ◊ ◊ ◊ ◊ ◊ ◊ ◊ ◊ ◊ ◊

Date:
Website:
Username:
Password:
Email:
Phone:
Security questions:
Notes:

◊ ◊ ◊ ◊ ◊ ◊ ◊ ◊ ◊ ◊ ◊ ◊ ◊ ◊ ◊ ◊ ◊

Date:
Website:
Username:
Password:
Email:
Phone:
Security questions:
Notes:

Date:
Website:
Username:
Password:
Email:
Phone:
Security questions:
Notes:

◇ ◇ ◇ ◇ ◇ ◇ ◇ ◇ ◇ ◇ ◇ ◇ ◇ ◇ ◇ ◇

Date:
Website:
Username:
Password:
Email:
Phone:
Security questions:
Notes:

◇ ◇ ◇ ◇ ◇ ◇ ◇ ◇ ◇ ◇ ◇ ◇ ◇ ◇ ◇ ◇

Date:
Website:
Username:
Password:
Email:
Phone:
Security questions:
Notes:

Date:

Website:

Username:

Password:

Email:

Phone:

Security questions:

Notes:

◊ ◊ ◊ ◊ ◊ ◊ ◊ ◊ ◊ ◊ ◊ ◊ ◊ ◊ ◊ ◊

Date:

Website:

Username:

Password:

Email:

Phone:

Security questions:

Notes:

◊ ◊ ◊ ◊ ◊ ◊ ◊ ◊ ◊ ◊ ◊ ◊ ◊ ◊ ◊ ◊

Date:

Website:

Username:

Password:

Email:

Phone:

Security questions:

Notes:

Date: ....
Website: ....
Username: ....
Password: ....
Email: ....
Phone: ....
Security questions: ....
Notes: ....

....

◊ ◊ ◊ ◊ ◊ ◊ ◊ ◊ ◊ ◊ ◊ ◊ ◊ ◊ ◊ ◊ ◊

Date: ....
Website: ....
Username: ....
Password: ....
Email: ....
Phone: ....
Security questions: ....
Notes: ....

....

◊ ◊ ◊ ◊ ◊ ◊ ◊ ◊ ◊ ◊ ◊ ◊ ◊ ◊ ◊ ◊ ◊

Date: ....
Website: ....
Username: ....
Password: ....
Email: ....
Phone: ....
Security questions: ....
Notes: ....

....

Date:

Website:

Username:

Password:

Email:

Phone:

Security questions:

Notes:

◊ ◊ ◊ ◊ ◊ ◊ ◊ ◊ ◊ ◊ ◊ ◊ ◊ ◊ ◊ ◊

Date:

Website:

Username:

Password:

Email:

Phone:

Security questions:

Notes:

◊ ◊ ◊ ◊ ◊ ◊ ◊ ◊ ◊ ◊ ◊ ◊ ◊ ◊ ◊ ◊

Date:

Website:

Username:

Password:

Email:

Phone:

Security questions:

Notes:

Date:

Website:

Username:

Password:

Email:

Phone:

Security questions:

Notes:

◊ ◊ ◊ ◊ ◊ ◊ ◊ ◊ ◊ ◊ ◊ ◊ ◊ ◊ ◊ ◊

Date:

Website:

Username:

Password:

Email:

Phone:

Security questions:

Notes:

◊ ◊ ◊ ◊ ◊ ◊ ◊ ◊ ◊ ◊ ◊ ◊ ◊ ◊ ◊ ◊

Date:

Website:

Username:

Password:

Email:

Phone:

Security questions:

Notes:

Date:
Website:
Username:
Password:
Email:
Phone:
Security questions:
Notes:

◇ ◇ ◇ ◇ ◇ ◇ ◇ ◇ ◇ ◇ ◇ ◇ ◇ ◇ ◇ ◇

Date:
Website:
Username:
Password:
Email:
Phone:
Security questions:
Notes:

◇ ◇ ◇ ◇ ◇ ◇ ◇ ◇ ◇ ◇ ◇ ◇ ◇ ◇ ◇ ◇

Date:
Website:
Username:
Password:
Email:
Phone:
Security questions:
Notes:

Date:

Website:

Username:

Password:

Email:

Phone:

Security questions:

Notes:

◇ ◇ ◇ ◇ ◇ ◇ ◇ ◇ ◇ ◇ ◇ ◇ ◇ ◇ ◇ ◇

Date:

Website:

Username:

Password:

Email:

Phone:

Security questions:

Notes:

◇ ◇ ◇ ◇ ◇ ◇ ◇ ◇ ◇ ◇ ◇ ◇ ◇ ◇ ◇ ◇

Date:

Website:

Username:

Password:

Email:

Phone:

Security questions:

Notes:

Date:

Website:

Username:

Password:

Email:

Phone:

Security questions:

Notes:

◇ ◇ ◇ ◇ ◇ ◇ ◇ ◇ ◇ ◇ ◇ ◇ ◇ ◇ ◇ ◇ ◇

Date:

Website:

Username:

Password:

Email:

Phone:

Security questions:

Notes:

◇ ◇ ◇ ◇ ◇ ◇ ◇ ◇ ◇ ◇ ◇ ◇ ◇ ◇ ◇ ◇ ◇

Date:

Website:

Username:

Password:

Email:

Phone:

Security questions:

Notes:

Date:

Website:

Username:

Password:

Email:

Phone:

Security questions:

Notes:

◊ ◊ ◊ ◊ ◊ ◊ ◊ ◊ ◊ ◊ ◊ ◊ ◊ ◊ ◊ ◊

Date:

Website:

Username:

Password:

Email:

Phone:

Security questions:

Notes:

◊ ◊ ◊ ◊ ◊ ◊ ◊ ◊ ◊ ◊ ◊ ◊ ◊ ◊ ◊ ◊

Date:

Website:

Username:

Password:

Email:

Phone:

Security questions:

Notes:

Date:
Website:
Username:
Password:
Email:
Phone:
Security questions:
Notes:

◇ ◇ ◇ ◇ ◇ ◇ ◇ ◇ ◇ ◇ ◇ ◇ ◇ ◇ ◇ ◇

Date:
Website:
Username:
Password:
Email:
Phone:
Security questions:
Notes:

◇ ◇ ◇ ◇ ◇ ◇ ◇ ◇ ◇ ◇ ◇ ◇ ◇ ◇ ◇ ◇

Date:
Website:
Username:
Password:
Email:
Phone:
Security questions:
Notes:

Date:
Website:
Username:
Password:
Email:
Phone:
Security questions:
Notes:

◇ ◇ ◇ ◇ ◇ ◇ ◇ ◇ ◇ ◇ ◇ ◇ ◇ ◇ ◇ ◇

Date:
Website:
Username:
Password:
Email:
Phone:
Security questions:
Notes:

◇ ◇ ◇ ◇ ◇ ◇ ◇ ◇ ◇ ◇ ◇ ◇ ◇ ◇ ◇ ◇

Date:
Website:
Username:
Password:
Email:
Phone:
Security questions:
Notes:

Date:

Website:

Username:

Password:

Email:

Phone:

Security questions:

Notes:

◇ ◇ ◇ ◇ ◇ ◇ ◇ ◇ ◇ ◇ ◇ ◇ ◇ ◇ ◇ ◇

Date:

Website:

Username:

Password:

Email:

Phone:

Security questions:

Notes:

◇ ◇ ◇ ◇ ◇ ◇ ◇ ◇ ◇ ◇ ◇ ◇ ◇ ◇ ◇ ◇

Date:

Website:

Username:

Password:

Email:

Phone:

Security questions:

Notes:

Date:

Website:

Username:

Password:

Email:

Phone:

Security questions:

Notes:

◇ ◇ ◇ ◇ ◇ ◇ ◇ ◇ ◇ ◇ ◇ ◇ ◇ ◇ ◇ ◇

Date:

Website:

Username:

Password:

Email:

Phone:

Security questions:

Notes:

◇ ◇ ◇ ◇ ◇ ◇ ◇ ◇ ◇ ◇ ◇ ◇ ◇ ◇ ◇ ◇

Date:

Website:

Username:

Password:

Email:

Phone:

Security questions:

Notes:

Date:

Website:

Username:

Password:

Email:

Phone:

Security questions:

Notes:

◇ ◇ ◇ ◇ ◇ ◇ ◇ ◇ ◇ ◇ ◇ ◇ ◇ ◇ ◇ ◇

Date:

Website:

Username:

Password:

Email:

Phone:

Security questions:

Notes:

◇ ◇ ◇ ◇ ◇ ◇ ◇ ◇ ◇ ◇ ◇ ◇ ◇ ◇ ◇ ◇

Date:

Website:

Username:

Password:

Email:

Phone:

Security questions:

Notes:

Date:

Website:

Username:

Password:

Email:

Phone:

Security questions:

Notes:

◇ ◇ ◇ ◇ ◇ ◇ ◇ ◇ ◇ ◇ ◇ ◇ ◇ ◇ ◇ ◇

Date:

Website:

Username:

Password:

Email:

Phone:

Security questions:

Notes:

◇ ◇ ◇ ◇ ◇ ◇ ◇ ◇ ◇ ◇ ◇ ◇ ◇ ◇ ◇ ◇

Date:

Website:

Username:

Password:

Email:

Phone:

Security questions:

Notes:

Date:

Website:

Username:

Password:

Email:

Phone:

Security questions:

Notes:

◊ ◊ ◊ ◊ ◊ ◊ ◊ ◊ ◊ ◊ ◊ ◊ ◊ ◊ ◊ ◊ ◊

Date:

Website:

Username:

Password:

Email:

Phone:

Security questions:

Notes:

◊ ◊ ◊ ◊ ◊ ◊ ◊ ◊ ◊ ◊ ◊ ◊ ◊ ◊ ◊ ◊ ◊

Date:

Website:

Username:

Password:

Email:

Phone:

Security questions:

Notes:

Date:

Website:

Username:

Password:

Email:

Phone:

Security questions:

Notes:

◊ ◊ ◊ ◊ ◊ ◊ ◊ ◊ ◊ ◊ ◊ ◊ ◊ ◊ ◊ ◊

Date:

Website:

Username:

Password:

Email:

Phone:

Security questions:

Notes:

◊ ◊ ◊ ◊ ◊ ◊ ◊ ◊ ◊ ◊ ◊ ◊ ◊ ◊ ◊ ◊

Date:

Website:

Username:

Password:

Email:

Phone:

Security questions:

Notes:

Date:

Website:

Username:

Password:

Email:

Phone:

Security questions:

Notes:

◊ ◊ ◊ ◊ ◊ ◊ ◊ ◊ ◊ ◊ ◊ ◊ ◊ ◊ ◊ ◊

Date:

Website:

Username:

Password:

Email:

Phone:

Security questions:

Notes:

◊ ◊ ◊ ◊ ◊ ◊ ◊ ◊ ◊ ◊ ◊ ◊ ◊ ◊ ◊ ◊

Date:

Website:

Username:

Password:

Email:

Phone:

Security questions:

Notes:

Date: ....
Website: ....
Username: ....
Password: ....
Email: ....
Phone: ....
Security questions: ....
Notes: ....

....

◇ ◇ ◇ ◇ ◇ ◇ ◇ ◇ ◇ ◇ ◇ ◇ ◇ ◇ ◇ ◇ ◇

Date: ....
Website: ....
Username: ....
Password: ....
Email: ....
Phone: ....
Security questions: ....
Notes: ....

....

◇ ◇ ◇ ◇ ◇ ◇ ◇ ◇ ◇ ◇ ◇ ◇ ◇ ◇ ◇ ◇ ◇

Date: ....
Website: ....
Username: ....
Password: ....
Email: ....
Phone: ....
Security questions: ....
Notes: ....

....

Date:
Website:
Username:
Password:
Email:
Phone:
Security questions:
Notes:

◇ ◇ ◇ ◇ ◇ ◇ ◇ ◇ ◇ ◇ ◇ ◇ ◇ ◇ ◇ ◇

Date:
Website:
Username:
Password:
Email:
Phone:
Security questions:
Notes:

◇ ◇ ◇ ◇ ◇ ◇ ◇ ◇ ◇ ◇ ◇ ◇ ◇ ◇ ◇ ◇

Date:
Website:
Username:
Password:
Email:
Phone:
Security questions:
Notes:

Date:
Website:
Username:
Password:
Email:
Phone:
Security questions:
Notes:

◊ ◊ ◊ ◊ ◊ ◊ ◊ ◊ ◊ ◊ ◊ ◊ ◊ ◊ ◊ ◊

Date:
Website:
Username:
Password:
Email:
Phone:
Security questions:
Notes:

◊ ◊ ◊ ◊ ◊ ◊ ◊ ◊ ◊ ◊ ◊ ◊ ◊ ◊ ◊ ◊

Date:
Website:
Username:
Password:
Email:
Phone:
Security questions:
Notes:

Date:

Website:

Username:

Password:

Email:

Phone:

Security questions:

Notes:

◇ ◇ ◇ ◇ ◇ ◇ ◇ ◇ ◇ ◇ ◇ ◇ ◇ ◇ ◇ ◇

Date:

Website:

Username:

Password:

Email:

Phone:

Security questions:

Notes:

◇ ◇ ◇ ◇ ◇ ◇ ◇ ◇ ◇ ◇ ◇ ◇ ◇ ◇ ◇ ◇

Date:

Website:

Username:

Password:

Email:

Phone:

Security questions:

Notes:

Date:
Website:
Username:
Password:
Email:
Phone:
Security questions:
Notes:

◊ ◊ ◊ ◊ ◊ ◊ ◊ ◊ ◊ ◊ ◊ ◊ ◊ ◊ ◊

Date:
Website:
Username:
Password:
Email:
Phone:
Security questions:
Notes:

◊ ◊ ◊ ◊ ◊ ◊ ◊ ◊ ◊ ◊ ◊ ◊ ◊ ◊ ◊

Date:
Website:
Username:
Password:
Email:
Phone:
Security questions:
Notes:

Date:
Website:
Username:
Password:
Email:
Phone:
Security questions:
Notes:

◊ ◊ ◊ ◊ ◊ ◊ ◊ ◊ ◊ ◊ ◊ ◊ ◊ ◊ ◊ ◊

Date:
Website:
Username:
Password:
Email:
Phone:
Security questions:
Notes:

◊ ◊ ◊ ◊ ◊ ◊ ◊ ◊ ◊ ◊ ◊ ◊ ◊ ◊ ◊ ◊

Date:
Website:
Username:
Password:
Email:
Phone:
Security questions:
Notes:

Date:
Website:
Username:
Password:
Email:
Phone:
Security questions:
Notes:

◇ ◇ ◇ ◇ ◇ ◇ ◇ ◇ ◇ ◇ ◇ ◇ ◇ ◇ ◇ ◇

Date:
Website:
Username:
Password:
Email:
Phone:
Security questions:
Notes:

◇ ◇ ◇ ◇ ◇ ◇ ◇ ◇ ◇ ◇ ◇ ◇ ◇ ◇ ◇ ◇

Date:
Website:
Username:
Password:
Email:
Phone:
Security questions:
Notes:

Date:
Website:
Username:
Password:
Email:
Phone:
Security questions:
Notes:

◊ ◊ ◊ ◊ ◊ ◊ ◊ ◊ ◊ ◊ ◊ ◊ ◊ ◊ ◊ ◊

Date:
Website:
Username:
Password:
Email:
Phone:
Security questions:
Notes:

◊ ◊ ◊ ◊ ◊ ◊ ◊ ◊ ◊ ◊ ◊ ◊ ◊ ◊ ◊ ◊

Date:
Website:
Username:
Password:
Email:
Phone:
Security questions:
Notes:

Date:
Website:
Username:
Password:
Email:
Phone:
Security questions:
Notes:

◊ ◊ ◊ ◊ ◊ ◊ ◊ ◊ ◊ ◊ ◊ ◊ ◊ ◊ ◊ ◊

Date:
Website:
Username:
Password:
Email:
Phone:
Security questions:
Notes:

◊ ◊ ◊ ◊ ◊ ◊ ◊ ◊ ◊ ◊ ◊ ◊ ◊ ◊ ◊ ◊

Date:
Website:
Username:
Password:
Email:
Phone:
Security questions:
Notes:

Date:
Website:
Username:
Password:
Email:
Phone:
Security questions:
Notes:

◇ ◇ ◇ ◇ ◇ ◇ ◇ ◇ ◇ ◇ ◇ ◇ ◇ ◇ ◇ ◇

Date:
Website:
Username:
Password:
Email:
Phone:
Security questions:
Notes:

◇ ◇ ◇ ◇ ◇ ◇ ◇ ◇ ◇ ◇ ◇ ◇ ◇ ◇ ◇ ◇

Date:
Website:
Username:
Password:
Email:
Phone:
Security questions:
Notes:

Date:

Website:

Username:

Password:

Email:

Phone:

Security questions:

Notes:

◊ ◊ ◊ ◊ ◊ ◊ ◊ ◊ ◊ ◊ ◊ ◊ ◊ ◊ ◊

Date:

Website:

Username:

Password:

Email:

Phone:

Security questions:

Notes:

◊ ◊ ◊ ◊ ◊ ◊ ◊ ◊ ◊ ◊ ◊ ◊ ◊ ◊ ◊

Date:

Website:

Username:

Password:

Email:

Phone:

Security questions:

Notes:

Date:
Website:
Username:
Password:
Email:
Phone:
Security questions:
Notes:

◇ ◇ ◇ ◇ ◇ ◇ ◇ ◇ ◇ ◇ ◇ ◇ ◇ ◇ ◇ ◇

Date:
Website:
Username:
Password:
Email:
Phone:
Security questions:
Notes:

◇ ◇ ◇ ◇ ◇ ◇ ◇ ◇ ◇ ◇ ◇ ◇ ◇ ◇ ◇ ◇

Date:
Website:
Username:
Password:
Email:
Phone:
Security questions:
Notes:

Date:

Website:

Username:

Password:

Email:

Phone:

Security questions:

Notes:

◊ ◊ ◊ ◊ ◊ ◊ ◊ ◊ ◊ ◊ ◊ ◊ ◊ ◊ ◊ ◊

Date:

Website:

Username:

Password:

Email:

Phone:

Security questions:

Notes:

◊ ◊ ◊ ◊ ◊ ◊ ◊ ◊ ◊ ◊ ◊ ◊ ◊ ◊ ◊ ◊

Date:

Website:

Username:

Password:

Email:

Phone:

Security questions:

Notes:

Date:

Website:

Username:

Password:

Email:

Phone:

Security questions:

Notes:

◇ ◇ ◇ ◇ ◇ ◇ ◇ ◇ ◇ ◇ ◇ ◇ ◇ ◇ ◇ ◇

Date:

Website:

Username:

Password:

Email:

Phone:

Security questions:

Notes:

◇ ◇ ◇ ◇ ◇ ◇ ◇ ◇ ◇ ◇ ◇ ◇ ◇ ◇ ◇ ◇

Date:

Website:

Username:

Password:

Email:

Phone:

Security questions:

Notes:

Date:
Website:
Username:
Password:
Email:
Phone:
Security questions:
Notes:

◇ ◇ ◇ ◇ ◇ ◇ ◇ ◇ ◇ ◇ ◇ ◇ ◇ ◇ ◇ ◇

Date:
Website:
Username:
Password:
Email:
Phone:
Security questions:
Notes:

◇ ◇ ◇ ◇ ◇ ◇ ◇ ◇ ◇ ◇ ◇ ◇ ◇ ◇ ◇ ◇

Date:
Website:
Username:
Password:
Email:
Phone:
Security questions:
Notes:

Date:

Website:

Username:

Password:

Email:

Phone:

Security questions:

Notes:

◊ ◊ ◊ ◊ ◊ ◊ ◊ ◊ ◊ ◊ ◊ ◊ ◊ ◊ ◊ ◊

Date:

Website:

Username:

Password:

Email:

Phone:

Security questions:

Notes:

◊ ◊ ◊ ◊ ◊ ◊ ◊ ◊ ◊ ◊ ◊ ◊ ◊ ◊ ◊ ◊

Date:

Website:

Username:

Password:

Email:

Phone:

Security questions:

Notes:

Date:

Website:

Username:

Password:

Email:

Phone:

Security questions:

Notes:

◇ ◇ ◇ ◇ ◇ ◇ ◇ ◇ ◇ ◇ ◇ ◇ ◇ ◇ ◇ ◇

Date:

Website:

Username:

Password:

Email:

Phone:

Security questions:

Notes:

◇ ◇ ◇ ◇ ◇ ◇ ◇ ◇ ◇ ◇ ◇ ◇ ◇ ◇ ◇ ◇

Date:

Website:

Username:

Password:

Email:

Phone:

Security questions:

Notes:

Date:

Website:

Username:

Password:

Email:

Phone:

Security questions:

Notes:

◇ ◇ ◇ ◇ ◇ ◇ ◇ ◇ ◇ ◇ ◇ ◇ ◇ ◇ ◇ ◇

Date:

Website:

Username:

Password:

Email:

Phone:

Security questions:

Notes:

◇ ◇ ◇ ◇ ◇ ◇ ◇ ◇ ◇ ◇ ◇ ◇ ◇ ◇ ◇ ◇

Date:

Website:

Username:

Password:

Email:

Phone:

Security questions:

Notes:

Date: ....

Website: ....

Username: ....

Password: ....

Email: ....

Phone: ....

Security questions: ....

Notes: ....

....

◇ ◇ ◇ ◇ ◇ ◇ ◇ ◇ ◇ ◇ ◇ ◇ ◇ ◇ ◇ ◇

Date: ....

Website: ....

Username: ....

Password: ....

Email: ....

Phone: ....

Security questions: ....

Notes: ....

....

◇ ◇ ◇ ◇ ◇ ◇ ◇ ◇ ◇ ◇ ◇ ◇ ◇ ◇ ◇ ◇

Date: ....

Website: ....

Username: ....

Password: ....

Email: ....

Phone: ....

Security questions: ....

Notes: ....

....

Date:

Website:

Username:

Password:

Email:

Phone:

Security questions:

Notes:

◊ ◊ ◊ ◊ ◊ ◊ ◊ ◊ ◊ ◊ ◊ ◊ ◊ ◊ ◊ ◊

Date:

Website:

Username:

Password:

Email:

Phone:

Security questions:

Notes:

◊ ◊ ◊ ◊ ◊ ◊ ◊ ◊ ◊ ◊ ◊ ◊ ◊ ◊ ◊ ◊

Date:

Website:

Username:

Password:

Email:

Phone:

Security questions:

Notes:

Date:

Website:

Username:

Password:

Email:

Phone:

Security questions:

Notes:

◊ ◊ ◊ ◊ ◊ ◊ ◊ ◊ ◊ ◊ ◊ ◊ ◊ ◊ ◊ ◊

Date:

Website:

Username:

Password:

Email:

Phone:

Security questions:

Notes:

◊ ◊ ◊ ◊ ◊ ◊ ◊ ◊ ◊ ◊ ◊ ◊ ◊ ◊ ◊ ◊

Date:

Website:

Username:

Password:

Email:

Phone:

Security questions:

Notes:

Date:
Website:
Username:
Password:
Email:
Phone:
Security questions:
Notes:

◊ ◊ ◊ ◊ ◊ ◊ ◊ ◊ ◊ ◊ ◊ ◊ ◊ ◊ ◊

Date:
Website:
Username:
Password:
Email:
Phone:
Security questions:
Notes:

◊ ◊ ◊ ◊ ◊ ◊ ◊ ◊ ◊ ◊ ◊ ◊ ◊ ◊ ◊

Date:
Website:
Username:
Password:
Email:
Phone:
Security questions:
Notes:

Date:

Website:

Username:

Password:

Email:

Phone:

Security questions:

Notes:

◊ ◊ ◊ ◊ ◊ ◊ ◊ ◊ ◊ ◊ ◊ ◊ ◊ ◊ ◊ ◊

Date:

Website:

Username:

Password:

Email:

Phone:

Security questions:

Notes:

◊ ◊ ◊ ◊ ◊ ◊ ◊ ◊ ◊ ◊ ◊ ◊ ◊ ◊ ◊ ◊

Date:

Website:

Username:

Password:

Email:

Phone:

Security questions:

Notes:

Date:

Website:

Username:

Password:

Email:

Phone:

Security questions:

Notes:

◊ ◊ ◊ ◊ ◊ ◊ ◊ ◊ ◊ ◊ ◊ ◊ ◊ ◊ ◊

Date:

Website:

Username:

Password:

Email:

Phone:

Security questions:

Notes:

◊ ◊ ◊ ◊ ◊ ◊ ◊ ◊ ◊ ◊ ◊ ◊ ◊ ◊ ◊

Date:

Website:

Username:

Password:

Email:

Phone:

Security questions:

Notes:

Date:

Website:

Username:

Password:

Email:

Phone:

Security questions:

Notes:

◇ ◇ ◇ ◇ ◇ ◇ ◇ ◇ ◇ ◇ ◇ ◇ ◇ ◇ ◇ ◇ ◇

Date:

Website:

Username:

Password:

Email:

Phone:

Security questions:

Notes:

◇ ◇ ◇ ◇ ◇ ◇ ◇ ◇ ◇ ◇ ◇ ◇ ◇ ◇ ◇ ◇ ◇

Date:

Website:

Username:

Password:

Email:

Phone:

Security questions:

Notes:

Date:
Website:
Username:
Password:
Email:
Phone:
Security questions:
Notes:

◊ ◊ ◊ ◊ ◊ ◊ ◊ ◊ ◊ ◊ ◊ ◊ ◊ ◊ ◊

Date:
Website:
Username:
Password:
Email:
Phone:
Security questions:
Notes:

◊ ◊ ◊ ◊ ◊ ◊ ◊ ◊ ◊ ◊ ◊ ◊ ◊ ◊ ◊

Date:
Website:
Username:
Password:
Email:
Phone:
Security questions:
Notes:

Date:

Website:

Username:

Password:

Email:

Phone:

Security questions:

Notes:

◊ ◊ ◊ ◊ ◊ ◊ ◊ ◊ ◊ ◊ ◊ ◊ ◊ ◊ ◊ ◊

Date:

Website:

Username:

Password:

Email:

Phone:

Security questions:

Notes:

◊ ◊ ◊ ◊ ◊ ◊ ◊ ◊ ◊ ◊ ◊ ◊ ◊ ◊ ◊ ◊

Date:

Website:

Username:

Password:

Email:

Phone:

Security questions:

Notes:

Date:

Website:

Username:

Password:

Email:

Phone:

Security questions:

Notes:

◇ ◇ ◇ ◇ ◇ ◇ ◇ ◇ ◇ ◇ ◇ ◇ ◇ ◇ ◇ ◇

Date:

Website:

Username:

Password:

Email:

Phone:

Security questions:

Notes:

◇ ◇ ◇ ◇ ◇ ◇ ◇ ◇ ◇ ◇ ◇ ◇ ◇ ◇ ◇ ◇

Date:

Website:

Username:

Password:

Email:

Phone:

Security questions:

Notes:

Date:

Website:

Username:

Password:

Email:

Phone:

Security questions:

Notes:

◇ ◇ ◇ ◇ ◇ ◇ ◇ ◇ ◇ ◇ ◇ ◇ ◇ ◇ ◇ ◇

Date:

Website:

Username:

Password:

Email:

Phone:

Security questions:

Notes:

◇ ◇ ◇ ◇ ◇ ◇ ◇ ◇ ◇ ◇ ◇ ◇ ◇ ◇ ◇ ◇

Date:

Website:

Username:

Password:

Email:

Phone:

Security questions:

Notes:

Date:

Website:

Username:

Password:

Email:

Phone:

Security questions:

Notes:

◊ ◊ ◊ ◊ ◊ ◊ ◊ ◊ ◊ ◊ ◊ ◊ ◊ ◊ ◊ ◊

Date:

Website:

Username:

Password:

Email:

Phone:

Security questions:

Notes:

◊ ◊ ◊ ◊ ◊ ◊ ◊ ◊ ◊ ◊ ◊ ◊ ◊ ◊ ◊ ◊

Date:

Website:

Username:

Password:

Email:

Phone:

Security questions:

Notes:

Made in the USA
Monee, IL
07 July 2026

56551663R00066